THOUGHTS ON CHURCH ORDERS

AND GOVERNMENT :

HISTORICALLY, ECCLESIASTICALLY, AND SCRIPTURALLY CONSIDERED.

BY

FREDERICK NEWMAN, D.D.,

INCUMBENT OF CHRIST CHURCH, FREE CHURCH OF ENGLAND, WILLESBOROUGH.

London :

HODDER AND STOUGHTON,

27, PATERNOSTER ROW.

ASHFORD : WILLIAM MILLER.

—

1877.

PRICE SIXPENCE.

THOUGHTS ON CHURCH ORDERS

AND GOVERNMENT:

HISTORICALLY, ECCLESIASTICALLY, AND SCRIPTURALLY CONSIDERED.

BY

FREDERICK NEWMAN, D.D.,

INCUMBENT OF CHRIST CHURCH, FREE CHURCH OF ENGLAND, WILLESBOROUGH.

London:

HODDER AND STOUGHTON

27, PATERNOSTER ROW.

Ashford: WILLIAM MILLER.

—

1877.

PREFACE.

———•———

IN publishing this little treatise, I am extremely anxious to have it understood that I have written, not as the representative of the Church to which I have the privilege to belong, but solely on my own responsibility. After many years of thought, and a considerable amount of reading on a subject of growing importance in these days of Church agitation, I have felt that a cheap book, embracing the pith of the controversy, might be useful to a class of readers who have not the time to read, nor the means to procure larger and far more valuable works.

I wish to acknowledge my deep indebtedness to the great and good men, living and dead, who have written on the subject, and from whose books I have drawn largely.

May the great Head of the Church bless this effort of my pen, and His name shall have the praise.

F. N.

CHURCH ORDERS.

———•———

WE live in a wonderful age—in a reading, thinking, active age. The knell of the first dispensation has long since ceased to be heard, and the life, the vigour, of the second dispensation now appears. It becomes us, therefore, to be good and wise—to " stand in our lot."

The political horizon gathers blackness — portends changes ; it may be storms are at hand.

The prophetical horizon is unfolding mystery ; the secrets of the Lord are being revealed in times and seasons, in days and months and years.

God Himself hath arisen and is working changes ; the kingdoms rage, constitutions are being altered, ancient institutions are ready to totter and fall to the ground, but " the Lord God Omnipotent reigneth ; " the future is known to Him equally with the past ; God will rule in righteousness, His truth is eternal ; principles will live for ever. The true Church of Christ is never in danger, " the gates of hell cannot prevail against it : " " The heavens and the earth may pass away, but my word shall not pass away." Zion is built upon a rock—the Rock Christ Jesus.

Some of the ecclesiastical institutions of our country are ancient. The Church of Rome boasts of its antiquity; the Church of England boasts of its antiquity, and the Free Churches in England claim antiquity the most ancient, because, as we think, the most in harmony with the apostolic and scriptural order.

We therefore dislike not antiquity; but, because a thing is ancient, we do not flatter ourselves that on this account it must be true. We take not such things for granted. If antiquity be false, we reject it; we search for ourselves the true way — that is, the scriptural — and endeavour to hold fast that which is good.

We study the fathers and follow them so far as they are like Christ and speak according to the oracles of God, and no farther.

" Whatever the Scriptures have instituted or directed is instituted and directed by God, and is invested with His authority. All else, by whomsoever said, or in what age soever, is said by *man*. But man has no authority over the conscience, and can never bind his fellow-man in any religious concern whatever. If, then, we find in the present or any past age anything said, whether by divines or others, however learned and esteemed, which is not said in the Scriptures, it is totally destitute of authority or obligation with respect to *us*. It may or may not be said wisely. It may be good or bad advice or opinion, but it cannot in any degree have the nature of law, or be at all obligatory on their fellow-men."

We love the truth of God wherever we meet with it, in whatever society it is found ; we wish not to constrain any man, but the Bible, and the Bible alone, must be the book of appeal. We ask only for that which to the fullest extent we are prepared to give to others—liberty to think and to act according to conscience.

We look upon the Word of God as complete in all its parts. Whatever is contained therein we feel bound to receive, and equally at liberty to reject whatever is contrary thereto. Now if a system, a peculiar, a special one was ever planned by God Himself, and intended to be binding on men, it is reasonable to suppose it would be clearly marked out in the Word of God. But if no such special-system be marked out in the Scriptures, *then* no man has a right to impose one upon me and bind me under pains and penalties to it. If God has not framed a scheme for me no person has a right to obtrude one upon me ; I have a perfect right with the Bible in my hand to compose one for myself, providing by it I do not infringe upon the consciences, the rights of other people.

I will now suppose that I never heard of any existing

Church order; I know nothing of ecclesiastical government, and am perfectly free from prejudice; but I have the Scriptures—which I believe to be authentic and inspired, the revealed will of God—and will proceed with my investigation.

Under the Old Testament dispensation I find there was a theocracy, a legal and ecclesiastical government, under the immediate control and direction of God, the nation itself sustaining by this means the twofold character of Church and State. *The Church* in its relation to Jehovah *as its God;* the State in relation to Jehovah *as its King.* In the administration of both these departments God made use of a system of supernatural interposition, and gave immediate manifestations of His presence and authority. He was the Head, the Guide, the Ultimatum; kings, rulers, priests, people, were alone amenable to Him; He blessed, He punished, in the Church and in the State.

Here the question arises, Can a theocracy be imitated? Is it at all within the range of mortal man to assume the place of the Most High? Was it ever intended that he should? And we answer, No. The thing is impossible in its own nature. A theocracy must be unique; wanting in one element it falls to the ground, it becomes a human device.

Under this economy, God adopted a nation (the Jews) as His peculiar people; placed His name, instituted forms of worship amongst them; manifested Himself in appropriate symbols, became Himself not only their God but their Judge, Lawgiver and King, assuming in a miraculous administration the reins both of civil and ecclesiastical authority.

And as there was the existence of this one ingredient in the Jewish establishment, viz., the *positive and absolute presence* and operating power of Jehovah, so there was the *absence* of another ingredient under the Jewish economy, viz., no such thing as *human* legislation in regard to religion: this is clear. It arose from the very fact of its being a theocracy. The laws both of Church and State were *Divine*—all from God Himself. The judges and kings were not *legislators*, for the laws were in the Pentateuch, in the inspired books of Moses; they had no authority whatever to enact a single statute of their own, or to abridge or alter those which had been laid down; they were only the executive, enforcing divinely enacted laws by divinely instituted sanction; they could neither introduce a new law nor a new punishment.

When, therefore, God was pleased to withdraw His miraculous and supernatural intervention, man had no means, no power, and therefore no authority to continue it. It was God's best plan for the age and genius of the people; but in the lapse of time, the Divine purpose having been accomplished, it was made to yield to some other plan still better adapted to the capacity and position of the people ; the theocracy was ended, and does not, cannot, in our estimation at least, form a pattern for a Christian Church, and is not recognised as a model Church in the New Testament of our Lord.

The theocracy being ended, there was a glorious appearing. In the fulness of time " God was manifested to take away sin." The government was to be placed on the shoulders of Him who was the Wonderful, the Counsellor, the Mighty God, the Everlasting Father, the Prince of peace, the Lord of life and glory "tabernacling with men." The great Head of the Church became also the great Teacher of the people. He introduced a new order of things ; the former things were done away, and the Gospel dispensation was introduced ; the kingdom of heaven was at hand, the true " Church of Jesus Christ." Here we may expect to find everything essential to the salvation, the personal improvement, and the spiritual edification of them that believe. He, the centre of attraction, who was come to draw all men unto Him, had seen the pattern of heavenly things, and His Church was to be differently constituted to that of the Jewish theocracy, to the Church in the wilderness.

The Saviour made a direct appeal to individual mind. Man was fully recognised as a personally responsible being, as accountable to God, therefore truth was commended to his individual conscience. Such language as this is re-iterated in his ears to show the personal application of god-liness to the mind: "What shall it profit a man if *he* gain the whole world and *lose his own soul?*" "*Ye* must be born again;" "Repent *ye*, believe the gospel;" "Come unto me all *ye* that labour and I will give *you* rest;" "For the kingdom of God is *within you.*"

As the Founder of a pure and holy religion, it was neces-sary He should openly and broadly state truths and lay down spiritual principles, rather than spend His time in forming religious organisations; especially as He under-stood so well the philosophy of the human mind, and knew that if He engaged individual mind and interested persons in saving truth, by the very laws of association and sym-pathy "like character would associate with its like," holi-ness of heart would ally itself to holiness wherever found. Hence He went about teaching the people, even from house to house. We say the Saviour laid a broad foundation in grand, fundamental, and everlasting truths. The great Head of the Church laid a foundation in Zion: the spirit-ual building upon it was to be gradually erected, com-posed of living, precious, polished stones, fitly framed together "for a holy temple to the Lord." Everything illustrated the personality of piety, the freedom of thought and the voluntariness of man.

Christ's reign was to be in and over the hearts of men;

it had nothing to do directly with the external order of Church systems or states, as such. His was "the kingdom of heaven" and "the kingdom of God." He Himself never intended, under this dispensation at least, to be a reigning monarch over countries or political parties, but to be the King of believing hearts, implanting spiritual laws in their minds, a reign of spiritual principles in their souls, which could co-work with all classes of men, and rightly and mightily effectuate His own purposes in saving and sanctifying "a peculiar people zealous of good works" amidst any system which men might devise—the spiritual King carrying on His spiritual reign independently of the laws of any earthly powers.

"The kingdom of heaven," as opposed to the reign of the kingdom of evil, sin in the soul; "the kingdom of God," as opposed to Satan, "the god of this world" and the tyranny of all wicked powers: Christ's kingdom as such had nothing to do with the establishment or legalising any national or state religion.

Organisations, associations, assemblies would almost of necessity grow out of the progress of the spiritual kingdom of Christ—the reign of grace in the heart and the advance of truth; but the nature and character of these organisms would be left in a great degree to the genius of the age and country in which the people lived, and through which holiness of heart and life would most conspicuously shine. The kingdom may be said to create the Church, but the Church must always exist for the sake of the kingdom. Hence, when our Lord was asked by Pilate (see John xviii. 33–36) the nature of His kingdom, He declared it was a spiritual one—"My kingdom is not of this world; if it were then would my servants fight;" as though he had said, "I have never legalised my religion, I have never mixed up myself, nor encouraged *my followers* to unite themselves with the state: the prerogatives of the two are altogether so different that they will not blend; you are legislating for this world, managing the affairs of time, I am labouring for eternity, setting up a spiritual kingdom in the hearts of men, which cometh not with observation, but with power; if one king comes against another it is with swords and spears and staves, but my kingdom is not of this world."

He asked only the individual, social, and moral elements of our nature to work upon; hence he says, "The kingdom of heaven is like a grain of mustard seed, which a man took, and sowed in his field: which indeed is the least of all seeds: but when it is grown, it is the greatest among herbs, and becometh a tree, so that the birds of the air come and lodge in the branches thereof;" "And where two or three are gathered together in my name, there am I in the midst of them." And that His Church, whatever might be the number, was to be composed of spiritual elements only, that those who constituted this body, the Church—managed their own affairs, is evident from the power He has expressly armed them with to expel offenders— "If thy brother shall trespass against thee, go and tell him his fault between thee and him alone : if he shall hear thee thou hast gained thy brother " (here is *personal* identity and *individual* responsibility recognised). " But if he will not hear thee, then take with thee one or two more, that in the mouth of two or three witnesses every word may be established " (*here we find fraternal* assistance, *mutual* co-operation). " And if he shall neglect to hear them, tell it to the church : but if he neglect to hear the church, let him be unto thee as an heathen man and a publican." The elect body made the final decision beyond which the offender might not appeal : " whatsoever ye shall bind on earth shall be bound in heaven : and whatsoever ye shall loose on earth shall be loosed in heaven."

Now, as Dr. Wardlaw says, " the whole of this Scripture relates to the same subject and contains the rudiments of Church government, the power of which belongs to the elect body." And we learn from it that nominal Christians have no room provided for them in the Church ; that when instances occur calling for the exercise of discipline, the members of the Church alone are sufficient to administer the discipline necessary, without the interference of any civil authority from without ; for it might happen that were a civil arm a part of the organisation of the Church, that arm might be the very part of the body requiring excision, an hypothesis by no means extravagant if the purity of the Church be an object; but, unless the power of excision be lodged in the spiritual community itself, this necessary spiritual purification could not take place; and it instructs us that a Church composed of only two or three is complete in itself; that like the human body it possesses a self-correcting principle and an expulsive power, and is fully competent to the discharge of its peculiar duties—"the body fitly framed together."

Wishing to influence the minds of men by truth and to gain followers from all grades of society, our Lord was progressive in His development of it and accommodated Himself very much to the circumstances by which he was surrounded and the character of those with whom He associated: He dispensed truth to them as they were able to bear it, and had no stereotyped course.

In process of time our Lord, needing help, chose twelve apostles and gave them commission concern'ng doctrine, but not concerning times, seasons, rituals; minor matters were left much to their own discretion—"Go ye into all the world, and preach the gospel to every creature. He that believeth and is baptized shall be saved; but he that believeth not shall be damned." "And, lo, I am with you alway, even unto the end of the world." Many felt it to be the power of God unto salvation and were added unto the Lord, even as many as believed. "Thanks be to God, which always causeth us to triumph in every place." It is true that they were opposed, bitterly persecuted, were scattered abroad; but all this turned out for the further-ance of the Gospel, "for the hand of the Lord was with them and a great number believed and turned unto the Lord."

The disciples still increased mightily, for on the day of Pentecost three thousand souls were added unto them, " and they continued steadfastly in the apostles' doctrine and fellowship, and in breaking of bread, and in prayers." Now this is very unostentatious it is true, but here, in our estimation, is the Church of Christ, *a model Church*—here are all the elements essential to Christian communion— and wherever these are found, there is the communion of saints, a Church of the living God, teaching apostolic doctrine; in other words, the Gospel of God's salvation, fellowship—*i.e.* the communion of saints, ordinances, breaking of bread, and prayers. *This*, I repeat, is Christ's Church, and what God hath joined together, let no man put asunder. Who, we would ask, can improve upon this for simple arrangement and solemn grandeur? and who will presume to alter it? Centuries have rolled away, hundreds of books have been written upon the subject, the fathers. so called, have spoken, learned doctors have controverted

the point, the question has been agitated age after age—
" What is the Church ? " " Hear the Church ;" "Where
is the Church ?" Let pompous pope, proud prelate, or,
histrionic priest point us to canons or creeds, to rites and
ceremonials ; let them lead us through majestic cathedral,
cloistered hall, or seats of learning to " hear the Church,"
and we pass through them all and hear the voice of antiquity indeed—the voice of truth, sounding from an upper
room—" These all continued in the apostles' doctrine, in
fellowship, in breaking of bread, and in prayers ;" and let
us meet with the communion of saints and listen to the
voice of prayer and receive the symbols of the body and
blood of the Lord ; let us hear of Jesus Christ preached as
the great Head of the Church in His prophetical, priestly,
and kingly offices ; let us see the Lord Jesus Christ evidently
set forth as the Way, the Truth, and the Life, and we care
not whether it be beside the rippling waters, on the top of
a mountain, in a private house, an upper chamber, or in
a splendid cathedral. Give us Christ, the Holy Spirit,
His Word, His friends, and there is the Church of the
living God.

The term Church signifies an assembly, a congregation
of any kind, and its being limited to a Christian assembly
is purely conventional ; for instance, it may be an illegal
or tumultuous assembly, as in Acts xix. 32: " Some
therefore cried one thing and some another : for the as-

sembly (*ecclesia*) was confused ; and the more part knew not wherefore they were come together ; " or it may be a legal assembly as in verse 39 : "But if ye enquire anything concerning other matters, it shall be determined in a lawful assembly " (*ecclesia*). In a religious sense as we now use it, it denotes, *first*, an assembly or society of true believers in Christ Jesus associated together in the fellowship of the Gospel (see Acts xi. 22–26) : " Then tidings of these things came unto the ears of the church which was in Jerusalem : and they sent forth Barnabas, that he should go as far as Antioch. Who, when he came, and had seen the grace of God, was glad, and exhorted them all, that with purpose of heart they would cleave unto the Lord." *Second*, The word Church stands for the whole company of believers (Ephes. i. 22) : " And hath put all things under his feet, and gave him to be head over all things to the church, which is his body ;" (Col. i. 18) : " And he is the head of the body, the church : who is the beginning, the firstborn from the dead ; that in all things he might have the preeminence ; " and *third*, it is comprehensively used to embrace the whole body of believers in heaven and earth : " Of whom the whole family in heaven and earth is named" (Ephes. iii. 15).

It is therefore manifest that little or nothing can be gained in argument by a reference to the original term ; but, whatever weight there is, is decidedly in favour of the polity we espouse.

The Church, in a religious sense, is the body of the faithful, a congregation of believing men and women (see 19th article); and there can be no doubt but that originally the elect body had the power to choose their own officers, to pay their own servants, and to manage their own affairs.

It is never hinted in the government of Churches that the right of governing is in the king or queen as the head, or in the bishops or deacons exclusively, but invariably in the Churches; that is to say, the members themselves, believers who have been added to the Lord and to each other.

We never read in the New Testament of the Church in a national form, as one corporate body compassing a nation or a province. Nowhere do we find in the Word of God the Church *of* such a nation; but invariably the Church *in*, or the *Churches in* or *of*; for instance, *in* Judæa, *in* Syria, *in* Cilicia; the Churches of Galatia, the Churches of Macedonia, arguing their distinctness from each other, their independence of each other, and at the same time their unity, cordiality and co-operation in the great work of the Lord. All the epistles are written by the apostles to the Churches with their bishops and deacons, and not to the king or queen as the head of the Church, or to the archbishops or bishops as the lords and sole governors of the Church. We have no Scripture proof of any political or legal authorities selecting bishops or priests for the Churches; but we have the most indubitable proof of believers, in their Church capacity, electing their own pastor, and setting apart their own officers to the work. And. indeed, this is conceded by all candid Episcopalians themselves; and the evidence in the memorable Hampden controversy is most conclusive on the subject, however little its spirit is acted upon and carried out.

The members composing the Church are called "faithful and chosen, holy brethren, the temple of the Lord, God's witnesses, lights of the world, fellow-heirs of the grace of God, the redeemed of the Lord. They are regenerated by the spirit of God, pardoned by the blood of Christ, justified by the righteousness of Christ, sanctified by the spirit of Christ, Christ's purchased possession, a holy brotherhood, fellow-citizens, heirs of the kingdom of heaven."

Evidently they possess a distinctive character: they are not of this world but are separate from it; they are to shine as lights in the world, to be the salt of the earth, to hold forth the word of life, to comfort, edify and build up each other in the faith of the Gospel. They are specially to make efforts to further the cause of God, to disseminate truth and to convert souls. Unto the Church of God is committed the word of reconciliation, "holding forth the word of life." My brethren, as believers, each of you have taken upon you the vows of God, each has spiritual duties to perform; and would to God we could awaken every Christian to a right sense of his spiritual responsibility; for none are answering the end of their fellowship unless vigilant, prayerful, sincere co-workers with God. And for lack of this our Churches languish, for we are comparatively feeble and few. We want an earnest and living Church, every member feeling his identification with the cause of God; and only let the people of God be aroused to a sense of their duty, to the cultivation of personal piety and Christian obligation, and we are confident our Churches will shine as stars of the first magnitude; we shall see them come forth "bright as the sun, fair as the moon, and terrible as an army with banners;" "the beauty of the Lord our God will be upon us," and He will establish the work of our hands. "God will bless us and cause his face to shine upon us;" "the word of the Lord shall have free course and be glorified;" the "handful of corn upon the top of the mountain shall shake like Lebanon, and they of the city shall flourish like grass of the field;" "the wilderness and the solitary place shall be glad for them, and the desert shall rejoice and blossom as the rose."

In the Church of Christ it is the privilege of believers to elect members for communion, and if needs be, to excommunicate them (Rom. xv. 7): "Wherefore receive ye one another, as Christ also hath received us to the glory of God;"

(1 Cor. v. 12) : " For what have I to do to judge them also who are without ? do not ye judge them that are within ? " (1 John iv. 1) : " Beloved, believe not every spirit, but try the spirits whether they are of God : because many false prophets are gone out into the world. Hereby know ye the Spirit of God ; " and " ye that are spiritual, restore such an one in the spirit of meekness." " Whatsoever ye shall bind on earth shall be bound in heaven, and whatsoever ye shall loose on earth, shall be loosed in heaven." And as there were neither popes, prelates, nor houses of assemblies in the apostolic age, there existed no organisation out of the Churches that could interfere with the self-government of them. The apostles themselves disclaimed all dominion over the faith of the brethren, they would not " lord it over God's heritage," and everywhere we find the multitude of believers were called together to deliberate and decide on questions pertaining to the Church of Jesus Christ. And who so fit to determine matters as the body of believers themselves ? Who so fit to carry out the designs of God as revealed in the Gospel ? Who so fit to govern, as the whole house " fitly framed together ? " And, surely, if the wisdom of one man is valuable, the deliberation of the household of faith must be better—far more valuable still. " The eye cannot say unto the hand, I have no need of thee : nor again the head to the feet, I have no need of you ; " " For all we being many, are one body and one

bread ; " " For as the body is one, and hath many members, and all the members of that one body, being many, are one body : so also is Christ" (1 Cor. xii. 12).

It is the duty of the Church of Christ to elect its own officers, and the permanent orders of a Christian Church are two, viz., bishops and deacons. The terms elders, presbyters, bishops, are interchangeable, referring to the same office. Indeed it is admitted on all hands, that the only permanent orders are bishops and deacons; the former to be devoted entirely to the ministry of the Gospel, the preaching of the Word of God, and the oversight of the flock committed to their care ; and the latter to attend to the temporalities of minister and people. " It was evidently not by an apostle's hands alone," says Dr. Jacobs, " that sacred orders could be conferred ; the authority to appoint Church officers was inherent in every duly constituted Church as the natural right of a lawful and well-organised society. And as presbyters might be joined with an apostle in ordaining, so might they without an apostle give this sanction of ecclesiastical authority in the ordination of any minister in their Church. And thus, not only Timothy and Titus, who were specially delegated by Paul, ordained presbyters and deacons in the Churches of Ephesus and Crete, but " certain prophets and teachers " at Antioch, without any such apostolic delegation were competent to ordain elders or presbyters.

The term bishop is synonymous with overseer or pastor, and involves no charge or duty distinct from those of elder and presbyter. They are never mentioned as distinct orders, for when elders or presbyters are named, bishops are not ; and when bishops are mentioned elders and presbyters are not ; in the New Testament, therefore, they are one and the same. And, in addition to the Scripture, all antiquity is on our side. Moshiem says, " The two terms, presbyter and bishop, were undoubtedly applied to the same order of men ; " Archbishop Cranmer says, " Bishops and priests or presbyters are the same in office ; " Bishop Burnet says, " I acknowledge bishop and presbyter to be one and the same office ;" Dr. Hammond says, " Presbyters or elders mentioned in the Acts and others places, were bishops ; " so Hooker, Dodwell, and most of the greatest authorities among Church writers. So amongst the fathers, Polycarp, Tertullian, Irenæus, Hilary, Theodoret, Jerome, and many others declare that bishops and presbyters are the same in office. So amongst the more modern, Lord Chancellor King, Neander, Doddridge, Adam Clarke, Campbell, Killan, Mossman, Jacobs, Barnes, &c. It is also equally certain from all these sources of evidence that, in the scriptural, primitive, and purest ages of the Church, there was no such thing as a diocesan or prelatical bishop ; all the ministers of Christ were bishops, presbyters or pastors, and had no difference of grade or rank amongst them.

" The episcopal office in its original institution was one of simple priority among the other ministers, rather than a superior order in the Church. Every town had its bishop with a body of presbyters and deacons under him; the Church often consisting of a single congregation assembling in one place of worship, and the bishop himself performing all the duties of a presbyter among them, and having a personal acquaintance with every member of his flock. So that the condition of each diocese, and the relation of its ministers to each other, were very much like what is now seen in one of our parishes in the charge of an incumbent, with several curates working under him and with him in it."

" Lord King, in his inquiry into the constitution of the primitive Church, declares that, during the first three centuries, each bishop's diocese, or rather his ' parish '—for it was then called παροικία (*paroikia*)—contained only one church, *i.e.* one congregation meeting in a single place of worship." Perhaps, however, this is too sweeping an assertion. Each Church or society, then, had a bishop or pastor over it: some few had more than one, but no bishop had any legal authority over the rest of the ministry. This distinction did not arise until about A.D. 150, and this, as the late liberal and learned Dean of Durham states, " was the beginning of the corruption of the clergy."

The statute of Queen Elizabeth, A.D. 1570, entitled, "An act for the ministers of the Church to be of sound religion," only requires those who had received ordination in any other form of institution, consecration or ordering than that of the Church of England to subscribe to the "Articles of Religion" in order to hold ecclesiastical orders in this country; no objection at all being raised to the validity of such ordinations.

It is proved by a great variety and a long series of evidence that, during the first hundred years after the beginning of the English Reformation, Presbyterian communities were recognised, and men who had only Presbyterian ordination were received, and obtained the highest preferments in the Church of England.

The characters of bishop and deacon are beautifully sketched by the Apostle Paul in his epistle to Timothy: "Must not be a novice," one newly planted in the Church of Christ, he must be of some standing in the Church before he is called to the office; his character must be approved, his gifts, graces, and conduct must be known and duly acknowledged. He must have a competency of knowledge and understanding in Divine things, so as to be able to teach others also; he must have a special and peculiar gift from Christ, hence he must not only be *able* but *apt* to teach, which aptness is not only in mental ability, but also in a good degree of elocution, a free utterance, the power of communicating with ease spiritual and intellectual truths ; he must be " blameless " in conversation, " of good behaviour, and have a good report of them that are without." He must not be given to any vice, he must be vigilant, watching over himself and his flock, taking heed of both. He, in a word, must have an *internal* and an *external* call ; " he must save himself and them that hear him." And that the Churches have the right to choose their own pastors and deacons is plain from Acts i. 15–26. There we find the infant Church assembled, but the number of the apostles was incomplete by the apostacy of Judas : it was necessary that another should be chosen to take his office. It is well known how any, claiming supremacy, would, under these circumstances, have acted; St. Peter, for instance, if he had possessed supremacy, would have asserted it as strongly as he who now claims to be his successor. He would have said, " Of our own proper motion, in our certain knowledge, and in the plenitude of our apostolic power, we have resolved and hereby decree " such and such things. Now it is very remarkable that in this " Church meeting " Peter *did* take a part, and that *he did not* take any such part as the Pope of Rome assumes to belong to him in the right of his succession and infallibility.

According to some of the fathers, Peter was the eldest of the apostles ; he did, therefore, what we should expect the senior to do and no more. Peter proposed the appointment of some one in the place of him of whom it was written, "Let his habitation be desolate, and his bishopric let another take." But having proposed this, *they*, not *he*, appointed; they, that is the elect body, the Church. They all—he with them, they with him, all on an equality—prayed and said, "Thou, Lord, which knowest the hearts of all men, shew whether of these two thou hast chosen, that he may take part of this ministry and apostleship, from which Judas by transgression fell;" then *they*, all on an equality, gave forth lots, and their lot fell upon Matthias; Peter was only one among many. Pass on to chap. vi. 1-5: the twelve called the multitude of disciples and said, "Look ye out among you, seven men of honest report, full of the Holy Ghost and wisdom, whom we may appoint over this business." Here you will perceive the brethren selected and chose, the deacons and the apostles appointed them; there was no supremacy, "for they [the apostles], when they had prayed, laid their hands upon them;" so Acts xvi. 21-23, and many others, showing the same course of procedure, indeed evidence is superabundant. Tyndal, in his translation of the Bible, says, "These seniors were ordained by election;" Beza says, "Pastors were chosen by the people;" Dean Waddington says, "Of most of the apostolic Churches, the first bishops or pastors were appointed by the apostles;

but, on their death, the choice of succession devolved upon the members of the society." Again he says, "This appointment was final, requiring no confirmation from the civil power, or any superior prelate; they constituted independent communities." Zonarus says, "Formerly bishops were chosen by the votes of the people;" Cyprian says, "The people have the chief power, either of choosing a worthy minister, or rejecting an unworthy one;" Bishop Lowth says, "The people in ancient times did choose their own bishops, and nothing but ignorance and folly can plead the contrary."

With respect to orders and ordination, it is important to notice the simplicity the Lord Jesus Christ observed in the election of His apostles. We see nothing of ceremony in it; no ordination service after the fashion of modern times; no "apostolical succession" spoken of; no gathering of clergy together; no parade of any kind; but simply a call to "come" and follow Him, and to "go and preach the gospel to every creature." It is true the previous night was wholly spent in prayer for His apostles ere He chose them; but it is not said He ordained them by laying on of hands, or, indeed, observed any special form. The words "ordain" or "ordained," as used in the gospels, do not imply any ceremonial, but simply making or appointing them to preach the gospel and do His work as witnesses for Him.

The apostle Paul knew nothing of a priesthood, of any "apostolical succession;" nothing of any conveyance of grace or gift by the laying on of hands to qualify men for the service of God; for, respecting baptism, he thanked God that he had baptized "none save Crispus, and Gaius," etc., "for Christ," said he, "sent me not to baptize, but to preach the gospel." He, therefore, was no believer in "baptismal regeneration;" and, with regard to his call and qualification to become a minister of the gospel, no sooner were his eyes opened at the words of Ananias, than immediately he began to preach the Lord Jesus Christ. It would seem he did not wait for any human sanction, no letters of commendation or dimissory; he in no way mixed himself up with the college of apostles, nor consulted them about the mission he proposed undertaking, but, under the direction of the Holy Spirit, acted quite independently. In proof, see Gal. i. 15-20: "But when it pleased God, who set me apart from my mother's womb, and called me by his grace to reveal his Son in me, that I might preach him among the Gentiles, immediately I conferred not with flesh and blood, neither went I away to Jerusalem to them which were apostles before me, but I went away into Arabia and returned back again unto Damascus; then after three years I went up to Jerusalem to visit Cephas, and tarried with him fifteen days, but other of the apostles saw I none save James, the brother of the Lord" (Alford's trans.)

The subject of ordaining ministers is mentioned nine times in the New Testament, four in the phraseology of *laying on hands*, and five in other varying terms.

That there was among the apostles and in the first Churches ordination, and by the laying on of the hands of the presbytery, to the work of the ministry we do not doubt. Paul appointed or set apart Titus as *primus inter-pares* at Crete specially to ordain presbyters (Titus i. 4-7): "To Titus, mine own child, after the common faith, grace and peace from God the Father and Christ Jesus our Saviour. For this cause left I thee behind in Crete, that thou shouldest further set in order the things that are wanting, and appoint elders in every city as I prescribe to thee: if any be under no imputation, the husband of one wife, having believing children who are not accused of dissoluteness, or unruly. For a bishop must be under no imputation, as being the steward of God," etc. (Alford's version.)

St. Paul had successfully preached the gospel at Crete, but was suddenly called away before he could organise a Christian Church; he therefore left Titus behind to set in order the things that were wanting, and to ordain, *i.e.* to appoint or constitute "elders" (καταστήσης πρεσβυτέρους) from city to city as Paul had directed, prescribing as well the *act* of constituting elders, as also the *manner* of doing so, which latter includes the qualifications required in a presbyter or elder presently stated (ver. 7–9). Those called "elders" in the 5th verse are called in the 7th "bishops" (ἐπίσκοπος); *elder* is the term of *dignity* in relation to the college of presbyters; *bishop* points to the duties of his office in relation to the flock as pastor. As long, therefore, as Titus remained in Crete, he was *primus inter-pares* among his co-presbyters, having no superiority of orders.

And there is something very solemn and appropriate in ordination, viewed in this light of appointment and dedication to office by the presbytery, and also on the part of the members of the Church who have called him to labour among them; but there certainly was not then, and is not now, any conveyance of gifts or graces, no spiritual qualification given either by episcopacy or presbytery to fit the minister for his work.

As respects superiority and degrees in orders, we have seen already bishops and presbyters are equal, and that they can alike perform the same functions; at the same time we believe it may be wise and good and have excellent uses for the clergy to elect a brother clergyman as an elder or overseer over them, and to go in and out among the Churches, as Paul directed Titus, to "set in order the things that are wanting," and to advise as occasion requires.

The question may arise, Is an episcopacy essentially

necessary to make an order of presbyters? We answer, Certainly not. Can there be no scriptural valid ministry without an order of bishops such as the State religion of our own country and the Romish Church demands? Most certainly there can be and has been from the beginning. Presbytery is the root of episcopacy, *it is an order;* episcopacy is *not an order*, it may be it is an office, and, *we* think, expedient; the one may grow out of the other, but I repeat it, the first is the foundation of the other; the presbyter is ordained to an order, the bishop is consecrated or dedicated to an office; the first has all the authority, the scriptural right of the other, however he may, by usage and lapse of time, have resigned it.

And here we may be permitted to say that in our judgment the constitution of the Free Church of England comes very close to the spirit of the New Testament and the usages of the primitive Church in its orders of clergy, viz., bishop and deacon; the former being made to include the two offices of presbyter and bishop.

In its declaration of principles, the Free Church of England says as to orders, " Guided by the New Testament and by the ecclesiastical polity of the primitive Church, this Church recognises only two orders of ministers, viz., presbyters and deacons. Nevertheless, the first order is divided into two distinct offices, viz., bishops and presbyters. This Church maintains the ecclesiastical parity of presbyters, whether episcopally or otherwise ordained, as a fundamental principle of its constitution." Again, " This Church recognises and adheres to episcopacy, not as of Divine right, but as a very ancient and desirable form of Church polity ; but, for the avoidance of any possible misunderstanding, it hereby emphatically declares its repudiation of the Romish dogma of apostolical succession in the ministry as involving the transmission of spiritual powers."

There is, we repeat, no such thing as apostolical succession, there can be no such thing ; had there ever existed such a succession, the chain has been broken again and again, and no historian has been able with any degree of certainty to make out a reliable record. Rome cannot make it out, for there were three professed popes claiming the tiara at the same time. From which came the true succession ? England must trace her present succession from or through Rome. Can she be sure that her orders came from the right source ? Besides, there was an ancient British Church, a Welsh Church also, with bishops dating nearly from the apostles' days, what kind of orders were theirs ? Are we certain that these were, in the sense of the Church of England, episcopal ? We feel it is very tender ground, most doubtful ; terrible evils have come out of such pretensions, and most fearful consequences have followed, in direst persecutions, even to tortures and to death.

One can only wonder at and profoundly grieve that such dominant and bold pretensions could be put forth by the professed followers of the meek and lowly Jesus, who declares, " My kingdom is not of this world ;" that such cruel, cold contempt has been shown to other orders of Christian men on such slender bases, whose orders are, to say the least, scripturally and historically as valid as their own. Let us hope that ere long a more enlightened, and therefore better spirit may obtain. Oh to have done with strife of party, the setting up of one class above another, of saying, " I am of Paul, and I of Apollos, and I of Cephas," but let us all say from the heart, " I am of Christ ;" "God forbid that I should glory, save in the cross of Christ Jesus my Lord." We have had by far too much already of the pride of orders, distinctions, separations ; we have all much precious truth to learn, and many things to unlearn ; there is much excellence in every system wisely adapted to meet the claims of all classes, suited to different orders of mind and status in society ; therefore let not Ephraim vex Judah, or Judah Ephraim, but let us most cordially welcome all who hold to Christ as the great Head of the Church, to the work of the Holy Spirit, the fundamental truths of the gospel ; with all our hearts let us seek to love all who love Christ in sincerity, and help them forward in every labour of love, feeling that none can belong to the real Church of Christ, unless "born from above," made new creatures in Christ Jesus, living under the influences of the Holy Spirit and walking according to Christ's command ; for "by this shall all men know that ye are my disciples, if ye have love one to another, and if ye love not your brother whom ye have seen, how can ye love God whom ye have not seen ?" Oh to feel no Church can save, no clergy, no baptisms, sacraments, orders can save; for neither circumcision availeth anything nor uncircumcision, but a new creature, and faith which worketh by love.

Has the thoughtful, candid reader gone thus far with us and not seen that the troubles arising in Churches in these days could not have arisen but for the disregard of the subjects of the foregoing pages ? Then why make so extraordinary a change ? As a rule, what can prime ministers, lord chancellors, heads of colleges, and sundry patrons, however conscientious, know of the fitness of the individual for the parish ? Who so qualified to exercise the right of choice as the Church over which the minister is called to preside ? Who so fit to judge of his qualifications as themselves ? Who so proper to elect as the believers among whom he is to live ? In what better way can confidence be gained, love be promoted, or prosperity expected ? We believe this to be the Divine method, and when rightly acted upon is found to work well alike for pastor and people. But then observe, out of this privilege most important duties arise to each member of the Church of Christ, viz., to know and to confide in their pastors, so as to communicate with them concerning the state of their souls ; to acknowledge them as their pastors in a peculiar sense in which other clergy are not ; to value their ministerial services and pastoral acts ; to love and esteem them highly for their works' sake ; to show a concern for their comfort and welfare ; co-operating with them in works of usefulness ; assisting in God's cause ; showing deep interest in the salvation of souls ; promoting the peace, harmony, and prosperity of the Church ; remembering that they are called unto holiness through the sanctification of the Spirit, and that they are " to show forth the praises of him who hath called them ;" to " work whilst it is called to-day ;" to " occupy " until He shall come, and so fulfil the law of Christ.

The Christian Church which we have been considering ought to be adequately supported and voluntarily. The voluntary principle is the only scriptural one, the only fair one, and it is the most ancient. No part of the Bible can be pointed to as sanctioning compulsion ; under the Jewish dispensation neither precept nor precedent can be found for exacting contributions from unwilling hands. It is true the priests received tithes from the people by Divine command, but there was no commission to compel them, the tithe itself being a voluntary offering. If a Jew was unwilling to pay, there was no legal punishment—everything was of free will. The tabernacle was raised by the voluntary, cheerful offerings of the people; and the temple itself, so magnificent and costly, was a monument of the power of voluntariness. "What am I," said David, "or what is my people, that we should be able to offer so willingly after this sort?" The system which rests the support of religion upon Acts of Parliament, or calls in the aid of the civil power, derives no countenance nor sanction from the Jewish Scriptures. Judaism, with all its imperfections and darkness, disowns and condemns it.

And if we come to the New Testament to find the will of God, we see He rests the whole support of His cause upon the willing contributions of His people; on no other subject is the will of Christ more plain. "The Lord hath ordained that they who preach the gospel shall live by the gospel." "Let him that is taught in the word, communicate unto him that teacheth in all good things." "If there be first a willing mind, it is accepted according to that a man hath, and not according to that he hath not." "Every man according as he hath purposed in his heart so let him give, not grudgingly, or of necessity, for God loveth a cheerful giver." "Upon the first day of the week, let every one of you lay by him in store as God hath prospered him." And this, to our mind, is the scriptural and literal plan of supporting the cause of God, which, faithfully carried out, would be sure to succeed. We believe there would be literally enough and to spare; in this way the stronger might help the weaker, and the poorest congregations might become strong and really efficient. Look for one moment at this plan; observe its universality—"every one of you;" its measure—"as God hath blessed you;" the time—"on the first day of the week;" the reason—"that there be no gathering when I come." We will not enlarge upon these thoughts, but let them be acted upon, and the voluntary principle would soon be felt all-sufficient, and peace and prosperity would obtain in our midst; the plan is simple, the offering easy, the work delightful as a thank-offering to God.

Thus, dear friends, have we feebly fulfilled our purpose and given you an outline of the Church which Christ has redeemed with His blood. In this Church we recognise Him as the sole, the great Head; we receive His doctrines, obey His commands, delight to do His will. As ministers we are to preach Christ's gospel; as members you are to receive the truth as it is in Jesus and to love it, to love one another with pure hearts, fervently, and thus glorify God.

And we need not say to our ministerial brethren that it is ours to minister in very peculiar times. " Who is sufficient for these things?" Brethren, our sufficiency is of God. Oh to be taught by the Holy Spirit; to be made wise to win souls for Christ; to be faithful unto death, that we may receive a crown of life.

> " 'Tis not a cause of small import
> The pastor's care demands;
> But what might fill an angel's heart
> And filled a Saviour's hands."

Let us aim, beloved friends, especially to convert souls, to edify believers, to build them up in gospel doctrines, and to preach them in the manner and spirit thereof; to extol Christ in his Divine and official character, setting Him forth as our Prophet, Priest, and King, the great High Priest of our profession, our Intercessor at God's right hand. Let us dwell much on the divinity and personality of the Holy Ghost, on the doctrine of the entire depravity of the nature of man, the utter inability of mere human agency, the absolute necessity of regeneration of heart, of the enlightening, saving power of the Holy Spirit, of the progressive character of piety in the soul, of holiness, of devotedness of heart and life to God. We do not say we want less of intellect in the pulpit, but might we not have more of spiritual savour, holy unction, spiritual point—in a word, more heart? We want not so much the elaborate essay, the finished, polished, magnificent discourse; people ask not so much for an intellectual feast as for food for their souls; they want not learned criticisms, but gospel sermons; not so much the opinions of learned men as to know the mind of the Spirit and the will of God. Neither, on the other hand, can they be satisfied with the drawling, aimless platitudes of some of the younger clergy, nor with the cold, formal, meaningless sermons of the ten, or at most, fifteen minutes' orthodox length; as though men's minds could be fed without knowledge, or immortal souls satisfied with so small a portion of intellectual and spiritual supplies—scant measure indeed, oftentimes little less than solemn trifling with eternal truths, immortal interests, and a holy God.

Brethren beloved, we think we see more clearly than ever, that, in order to do good, there must be primitive simplicity, godly sincerity, spiritual earnestness, the pure word of life. "And I," says Christ, "if I be lifted up, will draw all men unto me;" "And as Moses lifted up the serpent in the wilderness, even so must the Son of man be lifted up, that whosoever believeth in him might not perish, but have everlasting life;" "Behold the Lamb of God which taketh away the sin of the world." And what motives may we gather from a believing view of Christ crucified? "In that day there shall be a fountain opened for sin and uncleanness;" "The blood of Jesus Christ cleanseth from all sin;" "He is able to save to the uttermost all them that come unto God by him;" "This is a faithful saying, and worthy of all acceptation, that Christ Jesus came into the world to save sinners," even the chief ; and " the Spirit and the bride say, Come."   Oh the wonderful attractions of the cross : go when you will you are welcome ; go as you are, you will be received ; go as often as you like, and behold a smile ; there is mercy to pardon, grace to help, power to save, and love to melt at the cross.

Could we bring together specimens of the different characters who have been saved there, what a sight would be seen !   There, the lame, the blind, the halt ; there is the poor, dejected, trembling soul and the sinner who has never been able to forgive himself weeping before his Lord ; but the voice of Jesus sounds : " Thy sins, which were many, are all forgiven thee ; go in peace and sin no more."   Oh, there is such a mixture of feeling, such a thrill of delight, joy unspeakable and full of glory ! Angels catch the feeling with rapturous delight, and say, " Worthy is the Lamb ! "

Brethren, we love to linger about the cross (not about the Church and its orders) as the central point of faith and of attraction.   There we have seen many blind eyes opened, many deaf ears unstopped, many lame made to walk, many dead raised to life again.   There we have heard the song of the drunkard turned to a hymn of praise, the voice of the swearer turned to prayer, the stoutest heart softened, and souls prepared for heaven, grace exchanged for glory. Yes, we have seen many under the sound of the gospel brought to God, but never one sent empty away, never one rejected, never a soul disappointed or deceived. There weeping has been turned to joy and heaviness to gladness of heart. There God and the sinner have been reconciled. There Christ has smiled with mercy; the Holy Spirit has given peace and joy in believing, and the glory of God in the Church has been felt and seen. We entertain a high opinion of the piety, the talents, the usefulness of the ministry of the present day ; we believe there never was a time when we had such a race of men, such an amount of sanctified talent, such an active, energetic body of faithful servants of the Lord, good ministers of Jesus Christ, sound in the faith. We have a ministry of which, under God, we may well be proud : men whose hearts are bent on doing good, and whose influence is powerful for good in the Church and in the world. We love the ministry, we love the Churches, we love our brethren in Christ. Be stedfast, unmovable, always abounding in the work of the Lord ; be faithful unto death, holding fast the form of sound words ; be instant in season, out of season, feed the flock over which the Holy Ghost hath made you overseer, and soon you shall have your reward —" Well done, good and faithful servants, enter ye into the joy of your Lord." Brethren beloved, let us be more than ever men of study, men of prayer, full of the Holy Ghost and of truth, not shunning to declare the whole counsel of God. Let us, amidst the aboundings of error, keep close to the Bible, close to the Lord Jesus, depending more entirely on the Holy Spirit; let us love our order of faith, stand by our freedom, love and cultivate the spirit of the reformers; let us, in a word, have more of the spirit of Christ, and learn to abide our time—to " stand in our lot; " the day of truth is dawning, the day of triumph is not far off. Christ is all and in all, that in all things He may have the pre-eminence. He is the great Head of the Church, the ever-living, all-prevailing King in Zion; His glory He will not give to another. He will secure the victory, and His own Church, the Church which He has bought with His blood, shall be complete; " He shall see of the travail of his soul and be satisfied."

What is required in the present day is unity of action, hearty co-operation among all classes of Christians. In most of our Churches we apprehend the minister has too much to do, and the members too little. Let us more than ever be co-workers, and join heart and hand together. The pastor ought not to do all the work himself; it is not to be expected that one man should do everything; there is a diversity of gifts, and each should be brought out. The minister in the study and the pulpit; the officers in the care of the Church and of the sick; the members in attending diligently the means of grace ; all strive to promote prosperity, to follow peace, to love Christ. and thus to glorify God. " All we being many are one body ; " we are brethren beloved, and the success of Christ's cause should be dear to all our hearts ; and if thus holy, devoted, happy members of the Christian Church below, hereafter we shall form one happy family in heaven. And what splendid scenes will there be presented to our view ! What consummate delight shall we all enjoy, what untold happiness possess !

" And I saw no temple therein, for the Lord God Almighty and the Lamb are the temple of it. And the city had no need of the sun, neither of the moon to shine in it : for the glory of God did lighten it, and the Lamb is the light thereof. And the nations of them which are saved shall walk in the light of it, and the kings of the earth do bring their honour and glory into it. And the gates of it shall not be shut at all by day, for there shall be no night there ; and I looked, and lo, a number no man can number, out of every nation, kindred, tribe and tongue."
" These are they which came out of great tribulation, and have washed their robes and made them white in the blood of the Lamb ; therefore are they before the throne of God and serve him day and night in his temple ; and he that sitteth on the throne shall dwell among them." Patriarchs

and prophets, apostles and martyrs, ministers and people, and "many shall come from the east and from the west, and shall sit down with Abraham and Isaac and Jacob in the kingdom of heaven."

Millions of happy infants, young men and women, fathers and mothers, brothers and sisters, husbands and wives, relatives and friends, "one whole family in heaven," with Christ and like Christ for ever, shall go "no more out at all." See how glorious the angels, how beautiful the spirits of the just made perfect, how complete the robe of righteousness, how dignified the crown, how perfect the harp, how sweet the song—"Worthy is the Lamb," victory through the blood of the Lamb—how lasting the happiness, for ever and for ever.

We think we see the beloved pastor and his flock welcoming each other in heaven: "Here, Lord, am I and the children thou hast given me." There, in glory everlasting, are no more sighs, no more tears, for God Himself "shall wipe away all tears from their eyes." Most blessed place ; most happy eternity ; where all God's children shall safely enter in and join the sacred host. "Unto him who hath loved us and washed us from our sins in his own blood, and hath made us kings and priests unto God and his Father, to him be glory and dominion for ever and ever. Amen." The grace of Jesus Christ is consummated in glory, the number is made up, the Church is complete, the one family is united, the Church of Jesus Christ is glorified with Him in heaven.

> " Oh, happy harbour of God's saints,
>   Oh, sweet and blessed soil ;
> In thee no sorrows shall be found,
>   No sin, no care, no toil."

UNWIN BROTHERS, THE GRESHAM PRESS, CHILWORTH AND LONDON.

www.ingramcontent.com/pod-product-compliance
Lightning Source LLC
Chambersburg PA
CBHW081527040426

42447CB00013B/3363